HSP·
CALIFORNIA
EXCURSIONS

It gets you there!

Greetings California!

D1737812

Lead the Way

Senior Authors
Isabel L. Beck • Roger C. Farr • Dorothy S. Strickland

Authors
Alma Flor Ada • Roxanne F. Hudson • Margaret G. McKeown
Robin C. Scarcella • Julie A. Washington

Harcourt
SCHOOL PUBLISHERS

www.harcourtschool.com

ISBN 10: 0-15-352190-2
ISBN 13: 978-0-15-352190-4

2 3 4 5 6 7 8 9 10   0918   16 15 14 13 12 11 10 09

HSP CALIFORNIA EXCURSIONS

Lead the Way

Harcourt
SCHOOL PUBLISHERS

www.harcourtschool.com

Theme 1
Follow Me

Contents

Decodable Story

Social Studies

Social Studies

Paired Selections

4

Science

Social Studies

Social Studies

Social Studies

Paired Selections

Paired Selections

Theme 2
One for All

Math

Social Studies

Science

Science

Paired Selections

Paired Selections

Lesson 6

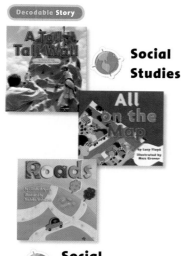

Social Studies

Social Studies

Themes 1 and 2 Big Books

The Lost Dog

Decodable Books 1–6

Comprehension Strategies

Before You Read

Look at the pictures. Think about what you already know.

Set a purpose.

I want to find out about frogs.

9

While You Read

Ask questions.

What do frogs eat?

Reread.

I'll read this page again.

Answer questions.

Oh! Some frogs eat bugs.

After You Read

Summarize.

First, tadpoles hatch from eggs. Then, they begin changing into frogs. Last, they are full-grown frogs.

Make connections.

This is like another book I read. I learned about how butterflies change.

Lesson 1 ➤

READING-WRITING
CONNECTION

CALIFORNIA STANDARDS
ENGLISH-LANGUAGE ARTS STANDARDS

Reading 2.2 Respond to *who, what, when, where,* and *how* questions.

Theme **1** Follow Me

Untitled, Maja Anderson

13

Contents

Lesson 1

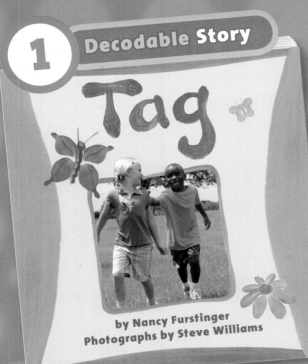

1 Decodable Story

Tag

by Nancy Furstinger
Photographs by Steve Williams

2 Genre: Nonfiction

Let's Tap!

by Alex Moran
photographs by
Sonny Senser

Good for You!
Toddler Rhymes for Toddler Times

original rhymes by Stephanie Calmenson

pictures by Melissa Sweet

3 Genre: Poetry

15

Tag

Phonics
Words with short
vowel a

Words to Know

Review

who

by **Nancy Furstinger**
photographs by
Steve Williams

16

Sam ran.

Sam can tag.

Dan can tag.

Pam can tag.

Pat can tag.

Who can tag Dad?

Sam can!

Focus Skill

 Make Predictions

When we read, we think about what might happen next. We **make predictions**.

Look at the pictures.

You can predict that the children will probably get on their bikes and ride away.

CALIFORNIA STANDARDS
ENGLISH-LANGUAGE ARTS STANDARDS—
Reading 2.6 Relate prior knowledge to textual information.

Look at these pictures. Tell what might happen next. Why do you think so?

Try This!

Look at the pictures. Tell what you think will happen next.

 www.harcourtschool.com/reading

Words to Know

let's

help

now

CALIFORNIA STANDARDS
ENGLISH-LANGUAGE ARTS STANDARDS—Reading 1.11 Read common, irregular sight words (e.g., *the, have, said, come, give, of*); **Reading 1.13** Read compound words and contractions.

Let's tap.

I can **help** you.

Now you can do it!

 www.harcourtschool.com/reading

27

by Alex Moran
photographs by
Sonny Senser

Nonfiction

Genre Study

In **nonfiction**, the pictures and words work together to give information.

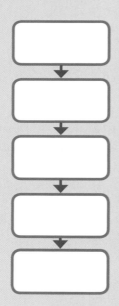

R2.2

Comprehension Strategy

Answer Questions

Answering questions as you read will help you think about what is happening.

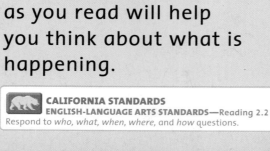

CALIFORNIA STANDARDS
ENGLISH-LANGUAGE ARTS STANDARDS—Reading 2.2
Respond to *who, what, when, where,* and *how* questions.

Let's Tap!

by Alex Moran   photographs by Sonny Senser

I can tap.

Can you tap?

I can help you.

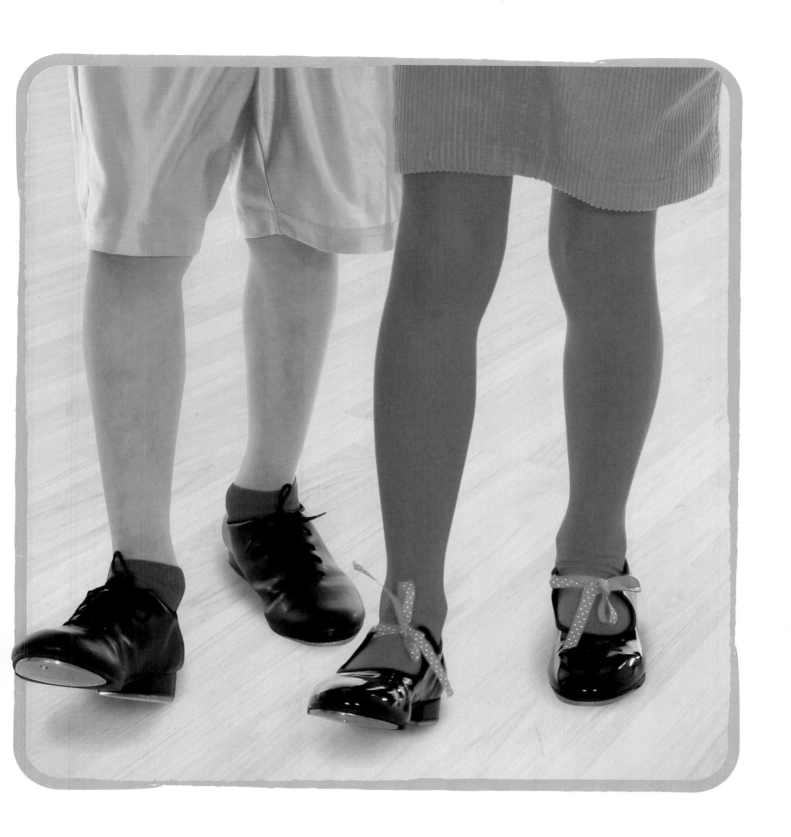

Tap, tap.

We can tap.

Can you tap?

We can help you.

Tap, tap.

Now let's tap!

Think Critically

R2.2
R2.6
R2.7
W1.1

1 Do you think the children will help others learn to tap? Why do you think that? MAKE PREDICTIONS

2 How many children are tapping together at the end? NOTE DETAILS

3 Do the children like to tap dance? How can you tell? DRAW CONCLUSIONS

4 How do the children learn the tap dance? MAKE INFERENCES

5 **WRITE** What would you like to learn how to do? Write about it.

WRITING RESPONSE

CALIFORNIA STANDARDS
ENGLISH-LANGUAGE ARTS STANDARDS—Reading 2.2 Respond to *who, what, when, where,* and *how* questions; **Reading 2.6** Relate prior knowledge to textual information; **Reading 2.7** Retell the central ideas of simple expository or narrative passages; **Writing 1.1** Select a focus when writing.

Meet the Photographer
Sonny Senser

Sonny Senser enjoys taking pictures, because pictures keep memories of his friends and family forever. Sonny enjoyed photographing this story. He says that it reminds him of how his niece and nephew love to dance in the living room when his family gets together.

 www.harcourtschool.com/reading

Wag, Hop, Hide!

by Stephanie Calmenson

Puppies wag.
Bunnies hop.
Kittens pounce.
Don't stop!

Birds flap.
Bugs crawl.
Turtles hide.
We do it all!

Connections

Comparing Texts

R2.2
R2.6
R3.3

1 Tell what you like about the story and the poem. How are they alike? How are they different?

2 Tell what kind of dance or movement you would like to try.

3 If you made up your own kind of dance, what would you call it? What would it look like?

 ## Writing

W2.1

Think about a time when you were in a performance. What did you do? Write a sentence about it.

I was in a show at school.

CALIFORNIA STANDARDS
ENGLISH-LANGUAGE ARTS STANDARDS—Reading 1.10 Generate the sounds from all the letters and letter patterns, including consonant blends and long- and short-vowel patterns (i.e., phonograms), and blend those sounds into recognizable words; **Reading 1.16** Read aloud with fluency in a manner that sounds like natural speech; *(continued)*

Phonics
R1.10

Make and read new words.

Start with **pat**.

Change **t** to **n** .

Change **p** to **r** .

Change **n** to **g** .

Change **r** to **t** .

Fluency Practice
R1.16

Practice reading "Let's Tap!" aloud with a friend. Read one page until you can read all of the words correctly. Then listen to your friend read. Continue reading until you can read the story smoothly.

Reading 2.2 Respond to *who, what, when, where,* and *how* questions; **Reading 2.6** Relate prior knowledge to textual information; **Reading 3.3** Recollect, talk, and write about books read during the school year; **Writing 2.1** Write brief narratives (e.g., fictional, autobiographical) describing an experience.

45

Reading-Writing Connection

Sentences About Us

"Let's Tap!" is about boys and girls who like to dance. We read the story. Then we wrote about what we like to do.

▶ **First, we talked about the story.**

▶ **Then, we named things we like to do.**

▶ **Last, we read our sentences.**

Student Writing Model

Zack likes to sing.

Hayley likes to play soccer.

Liz likes to read.

Beto likes to draw.

Contents

Lesson 2

1 Decodable Story

Sad, Sad Dan

by Guadalupe V. Lopez   illustrated by Valeria Petrone

2 Genre: Fantasy

The Van
by Holly Keller

People Movers

3 Genre: Nonfiction

Phonics
Words with short vowel <u>a</u>

Words to Know

Review

look

Sad, Sad Dan

by Guadalupe V. Lopez

illustrated by Valeria Petrone

I am Dan.

I am a sad, sad cat.

Look at Pam.

Pam has bags.

Pam has mats.

Pam has hats.

Am I a sad, sad cat?

Focus Skill

Make Predictions

You can **make predictions** about a story. Use what you learn from the story and what you know from real life.

Look at these pictures.

You can use what you see and what you know. You can predict that the girl will probably take a bite of her food.

CALIFORNIA STANDARDS
ENGLISH-LANGUAGE ARTS STANDARDS—
Reading 2.6 Relate prior knowledge to textual information.

Look at these pictures. Tell what might happen next. Why do you think so?

Try This!

Look at the pictures. Draw a picture to show what you think will happen next.

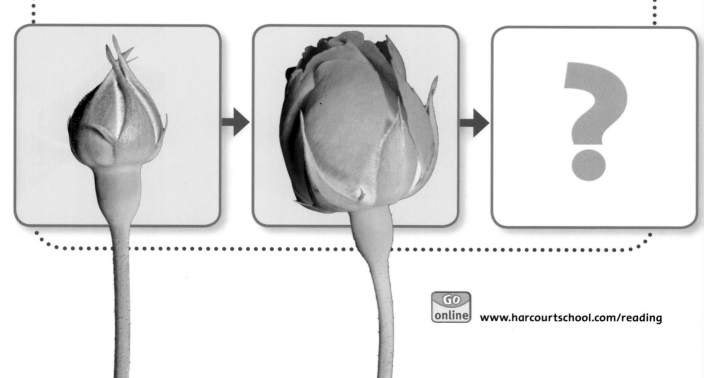

GO online   www.harcourtschool.com/reading

Words to Know

High-Frequency Words

R1.11

in

too

no

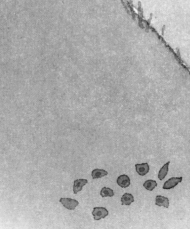

CALIFORNIA STANDARDS
ENGLISH-LANGUAGE ARTS STANDARDS—Reading 1.11 Read common, irregular sight words (e.g., *the, have, said, come, give, of*).

I sat **in** the van.

They sat, **too**.

Can we go? **No**!

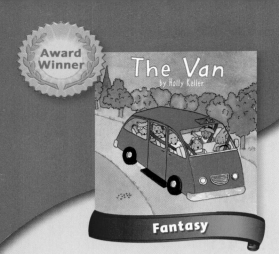

The Van
by Holly Keller

Fantasy

Genre Study

A **fantasy** story has parts that could never happen in real life.

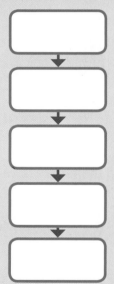

R2.2

Comprehension Strategy

Ask Questions As you read, ask yourself questions. Asking questions will help you think about what you are reading.

CALIFORNIA STANDARDS
ENGLISH-LANGUAGE ARTS STANDARDS—Reading 2.2
Respond to *who, what, when, where,* and *how* questions.

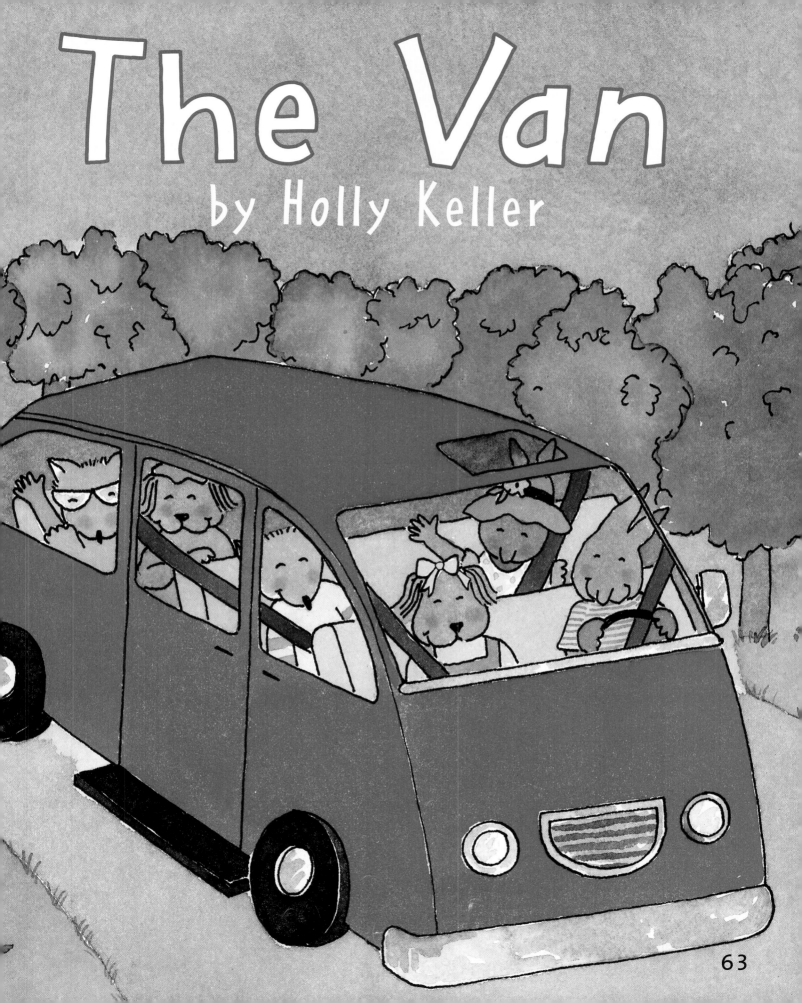

The Van
by Holly Keller

Sam has a van.

Pam sat in the van.

Max sat, too.

Dan sat in the van.

Pat sat, too.

Can the van go?

No!

Jan can help.

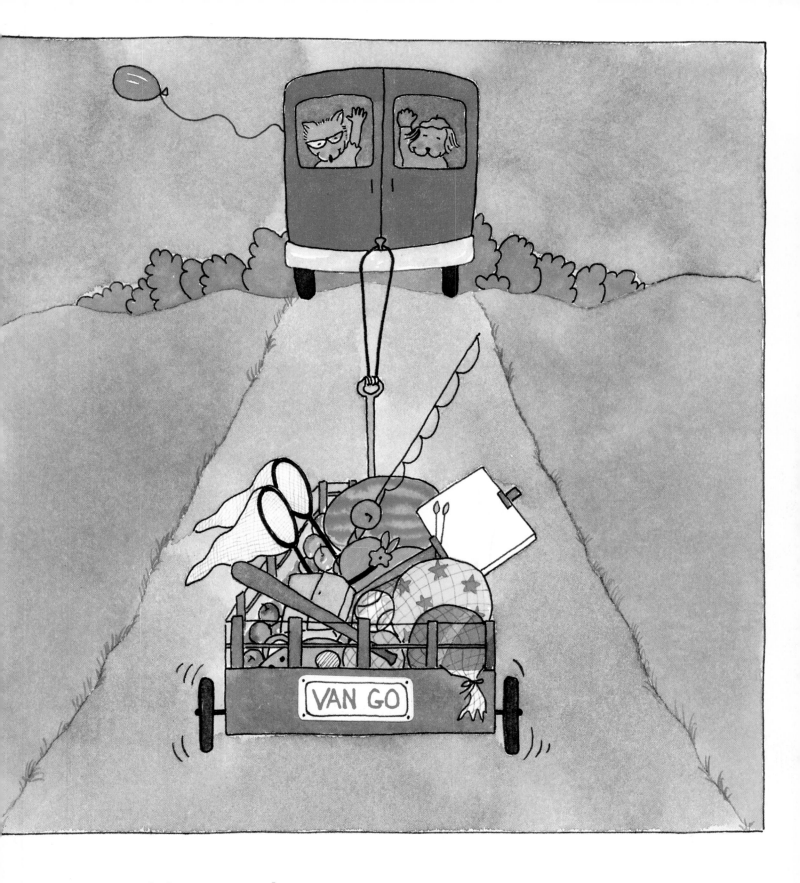

Now the van can go.

Think Critically

R2.2
R2.6
R2.7
R3.1
W2.1

1 Where do you think the animals are going? Why do you think that?

MAKE PREDICTIONS

2 What happens when Sam's friends put all their things in his van? CAUSE-EFFECT

3 Who solves the problem? How?

PROBLEM/SOLUTION

4 Could this story really happen in real life? Why or why not? FANTASY/REALITY

5 **WRITE** Do you like this story? Write about it. WRITING RESPONSE

CALIFORNIA STANDARDS
ENGLISH-LANGUAGE ARTS STANDARDS—Reading 2.2 Respond to *who, what, when, where,* and *how* questions; **Reading 2.6** Relate prior knowledge to textual information; **Reading 2.7** Retell the central ideas of simple expository or narrative passages; **Reading 3.1** Identify and describe the elements of plot, setting, and character(s) in a story, as well as the story's beginning, middle, and ending; **Writing 2.1** Write brief narratives (e.g., fictional, autobiographical) describing an experience.

74

Meet the Author/Illustrator
Holly Keller

Holly Keller loves to draw animals doing things that people might do. She never had any pets growing up but says animals are more fun to draw. She gets her story ideas from things she did as a child and things her own children did. She says that children's lives are full of stories.

People Movers

Nonfiction

Teacher Read-Aloud

People Movers

People move from place to place.

Sleds help us move through ice and snow.

Boats help us move through the water.

Special trucks help us move through sand and rocks.

Connections

Comparing Texts

R2.2
R2.6
R3.1
R3.3

1 How would "The Van" be different if Sam had a boat from "People Movers"?

2 "The Van" and "Let's Tap!" have friends helping each other. How have you helped a friend?

3 Tell about an activity that you would like to do with your friends.

Writing

W2.1 W2.2

In "The Van," Sam and his friends bring their favorite things with them. Think of what you would bring and why. Write about it.

I would bring my kite.
Kites are fun.

CALIFORNIA STANDARDS
ENGLISH-LANGUAGE ARTS STANDARDS—Reading 1.10 Generate the sounds from all the letters and letter patterns, including consonant blends and long- and short-vowel patterns (i.e., phonograms), and blend those sounds into recognizable words; **Reading 1.16** Read aloud with fluency in a manner that sounds like natural speech; *(continued)*

Phonics

Make and read new words.

Start with **<u>mat</u>**.

Change | t | to | p |.

Change | m | to | n |.

Change | n | to | c |.

Change | p | to | t |.

Fluency Practice

Read "The Van" to yourself. Then reread it with a friend. Take turns reading aloud until you can read the words correctly and easily.

Reading 2.2 Respond to *who, what, when, where,* and *how* questions; **Reading 2.6** Relate prior knowledge to textual information; **Reading 3.1** Identify and describe the elements of plot, setting, and character(s) in a story, as well as the story's beginning, middle, and ending; **Reading 3.3** Recollect, talk, and write about books read during the school year; **Writing 2.1** Write brief narratives (e.g., fictional, autobiographical) describing an experience; **Writing 2.2** Write brief expository descriptions of a real object, person, place, or event, using sensory details.

Contents

Lesson 3

1 Decodable Story

Miss Jill
by Anne Mansk
photographs by
Doug Dukane

2 Genre: Nonfiction

Big Rigs
by Paulette R. Novak
photographs by
Doug Dukane

Trailer Truck
by Bobbi Katz
illustrated by
Bob Staake

3 Genre: Poetry

Phonics
Words with short
vowel i

Words to Know

Review

now

let's

Miss Jill

by Anne Mansk

photographs by
Doug Dukane

Miss Jill has milk.

Miss Jill sits in a rig.

The milk is in bins.

Dan will fill the rig.

Dan will fit it in.

Now kids have milk.

Let's have a big sip!

Phonics Skill

Short Vowel i R1.10

The letter **i** can stand for the sound at the beginning of **it** and in the middle of **mix**. This sound is called the short **i** sound.

Name these pictures. Each word has the short **i** sound.

hill

pin

lid

kit

hip

six

CALIFORNIA STANDARDS
ENGLISH-LANGUAGE ARTS STANDARDS—Reading 1.10 Generate the sounds from all the letters and letter patterns, including consonant blends and long- and short-vowel patterns (i.e., phonograms), and blend those sounds into recognizable words.

Read each sentence. Choose the picture that goes with the sentence.

It is big.

Jill will fill it.

GO online   www.harcourtschool.com/reading

Try This!

Write **it** and **sit**. Write more words with the short **i** sound. Write a sentence with some of the words.

it

sit

Words to Know

High-Frequency Words

R1.11

so

hold

get

home

soon

CALIFORNIA STANDARDS
ENGLISH-LANGUAGE ARTS STANDARDS—Reading 1.11 Read common, irregular sight words (e.g., *the, have, said, come, give, of*).

This is **so** big!

Look what it can **hold**!

It will **get home soon**.

www.harcourtschool.com/reading

Big Rigs

by Paulette R. Novak

photographs by
Doug Dukane

Nonfiction

Genre Study

In **nonfiction**, words and photographs can work together to give information.

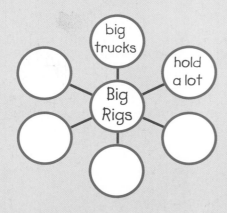

big trucks

hold a lot

Big Rigs

R2.6

Comprehension Strategy

Monitor Comprehension: Make Inferences As you read, think about what you are learning and what you already know. This will help you understand what you read.

CALIFORNIA STANDARDS
ENGLISH-LANGUAGE ARTS STANDARDS—Reading 2.6
Relate prior knowledge to textual information.

Big Rigs

by Paulette R. Novak
photographs
by Doug Dukane

This is my dad.

This is his big rig.

Big rigs are so big.

FIRE EXTINGUISHER INSIDE

Look at what big rigs can hold!

Dad sits in his big rig.

Fill it up!

Now Dad will go.

Get home soon, Dad.

Think Critically

R2.1
R2.2
R2.6
R2.7
W2.2

1 What is a big rig? CLASSIFY/CATEGORIZE

2 What do big rigs do? MAIN IDEA

3 Where do you think the big rig in the selection is going? DRAW CONCLUSIONS

4 If you could meet the people in the selection, what questions would you ask them? PERSONAL RESPONSE

5 **WRITE** When you grow up, what job would you like? Write about it.

WRITING RESPONSE

CALIFORNIA STANDARDS
ENGLISH-LANGUAGE ARTS STANDARDS—Reading 2.1 Identify text that uses sequence or other logical order; **Reading 2.2** Respond to *who, what, when, where,* and *how* questions; **Reading 2.6** Relate prior knowledge to textual information; **Reading 2.7** Retell the central ideas of simple expository or narrative passages; **Writing 2.2** Write brief expository descriptions of a real object, person, place, or event, using sensory details.

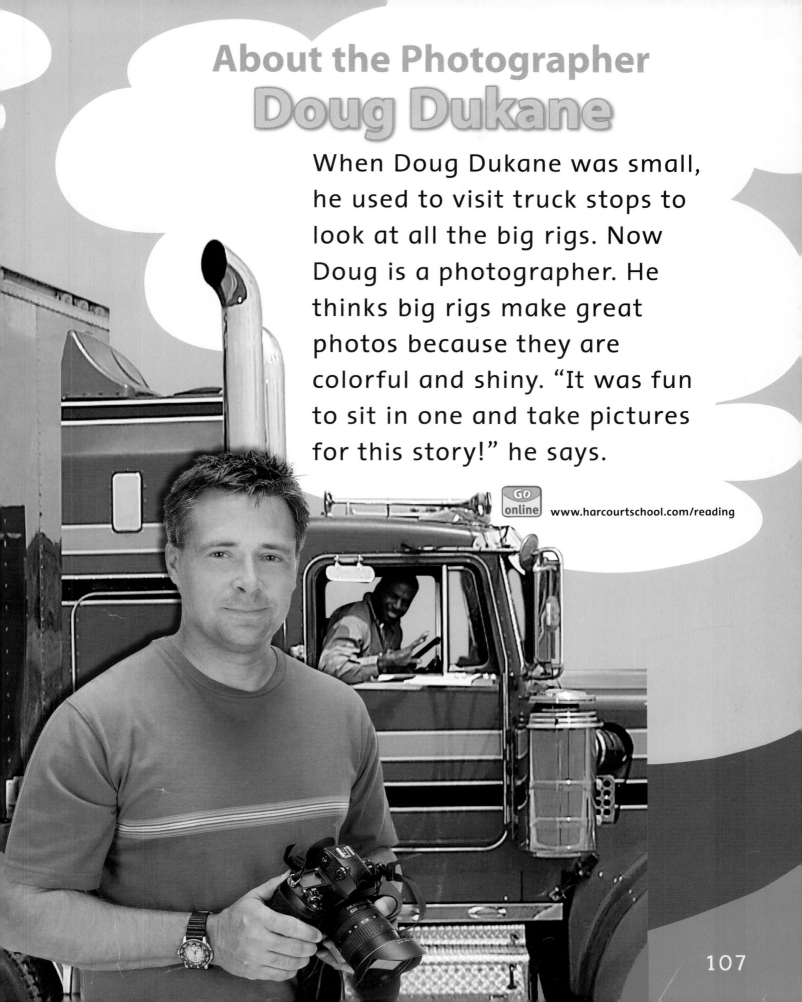

About the Photographer
Doug Dukane

When Doug Dukane was small, he used to visit truck stops to look at all the big rigs. Now Doug is a photographer. He thinks big rigs make great photos because they are colorful and shiny. "It was fun to sit in one and take pictures for this story!" he says.

GO online www.harcourtschool.com/reading

Trailer Truck

by **Bobbi Katz**
illustrated by **Bob Staake**

We are buddies. What a pair!
We go together everywhere.
What's a cab without a trailer?
Like a ship without a sailor!

We whiz along the interstate.
From coast to coast, we carry freight.
Oh, how wonderful it feels
to roll along on eighteen wheels!

108

Connections

Comparing Texts

R2.2
R2.6
R3.3

❶ How are the story and the poem alike? How are they different?

❷ What is your favorite kind of truck? Why?

❸ The cab and the trailer are buddies in the poem. Think about one of your friends. Tell what you like to do together.

Writing

W2.2

Think about "Big Rigs." Make a list of things that a truck might haul from place to place. Choose one thing and write a sentence about it.

A truck can bring apples to the store.

CALIFORNIA STANDARDS
ENGLISH-LANGUAGE ARTS STANDARDS—Reading 1.10 Generate the sounds from all the letters and letter patterns, including consonant blends and long- and short-vowel patterns (i.e., phonograms), and blend those sounds into *(continued)*

Phonics

Make and read new words.

Start with **<u>wig</u>**.

Change **g** to **n**.

Change **w** to **t**.

Change **n** to **p**.

Change **t** to **r**.

Fluency Practice

Read "Big Rigs" aloud. Remember to look at capital letters, commas, and end marks. This will help you know how to read aloud each sentence. Make your voice sound like you are talking to someone.

recognizable words; **Reading 1.16** Read aloud with fluency in a manner that sounds like natural speech; **Reading 2.2** Respond to *who, what, when, where,* and *how* questions; **Reading 2.6** Relate prior knowledge to textual information; **Reading 3.3** Recollect, talk, and write about books read during the school year; **Writing 2.2** Write brief expository descriptions of a real object, person, place, or event, using sensory details.

Lesson 4

Selection Titles	Pick a Sack **Get Up, Rick!** Cock-a-Doodle-Doo
Comprehension Strategies	Summarize
Focus Skill	Beginning, Middle, Ending

 CALIFORNIA STANDARDS
ENGLISH-LANGUAGE ARTS STANDARDS

 Reading 2.7 Retell the central ideas of simple expository or narrative passages; **Reading 3.1** Identify and describe the elements of plot, setting, and character(s) in a story, as well as the story's beginning, middle, and ending.

Theme 2 One for All

Instrumental Zoo II, artist unknown

Lesson 5 ▶

Jobs
Dot and Bob
Trees Help

Recognize Story Structure

Characters

Reading 3.1 Identify and describe the elements of plot, setting, and character(s) in a story, as well as the story's beginning, middle, and ending.

Lesson 6 ▶

A Tall, Tall Wall
All on the Map
Roads

Adjust Reading Rate

Words with <u>all</u>

Reading 1.10 Generate the sounds from all the letters and letter patterns, including consonant blends and long- and short-vowel patterns (i.e., phonograms), and blend those sounds into recognizable words; Reading 1.15 Read common word families (e.g., -ite, -ate).

113

Contents

Lesson 4

1 Decodable Story

Pick a Sack

by Linda Barr

illustrated by Laurence Cleyet-Merle

2 Genre: Fantasy

Get Up, Rick!

by F. Isabel Campoy
illustrated by Bernard Adnet

Cock-a-Doodle-Doo

3 Genre: Nonfiction

Pick a Sack

by Linda Barr

illustrated by
Laurence Cleyet-Merle

Nick has sacks.

Pick a sack, Jack.

Pick a sack, Mack.

Jack has his sack.

Mack has his sack, too.

Jack and Mack have gifts!

Kick it, Jack and Mack!

Focus Skill

Beginning, Middle, Ending R3.1

Stories have a **beginning**, a **middle**, and an **ending**. This order helps stories make sense.

Look at these pictures. They tell a story.

These pictures show the beginning, middle, and ending of a story about the girl.

CALIFORNIA STANDARDS
ENGLISH-LANGUAGE ARTS STANDARDS—Reading 3.1 Identify and describe the elements of plot, setting, and character(s) in a story, as well as the story's beginning, middle, and ending.

These pictures tell a story, too. What happens in the beginning, the middle, and the ending?

Try This!

Put these pictures in order. Tell what happens in the beginning, the middle, and the ending.

 www.harcourtschool.com/reading

Words to Know

High-Frequency Words

R1.11

oh

late

yes

CALIFORNIA STANDARDS
ENGLISH-LANGUAGE ARTS STANDARDS—Reading 1.11 Read common, irregular sight words (e.g., *the, have, said, come, give, of*).

Oh, no! It is **late**!

Is he sick?

Will he get up?

Yes, he will.

www.harcourtschool.com/reading

127

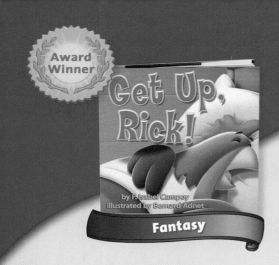

Award Winner

Get Up, Rick!

by F. Isabel Campoy
illustrated by Bernard Adnet

Fantasy

Genre Study

A **fantasy** story has parts that could not happen in real life. In many fantasy stories, animal characters talk and act like people.

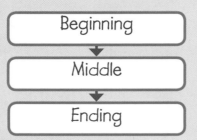

Beginning
↓
Middle
↓
Ending

R2.7

Comprehension Strategy

Summarize After you read several pages of a story, stop and think about what has happened so far. Summarizing parts of a story will help you understand and remember the whole story.

CALIFORNIA STANDARDS
ENGLISH-LANGUAGE ARTS STANDARDS—
Reading 2.7 Retell the central ideas of simple expository or narrative passages.

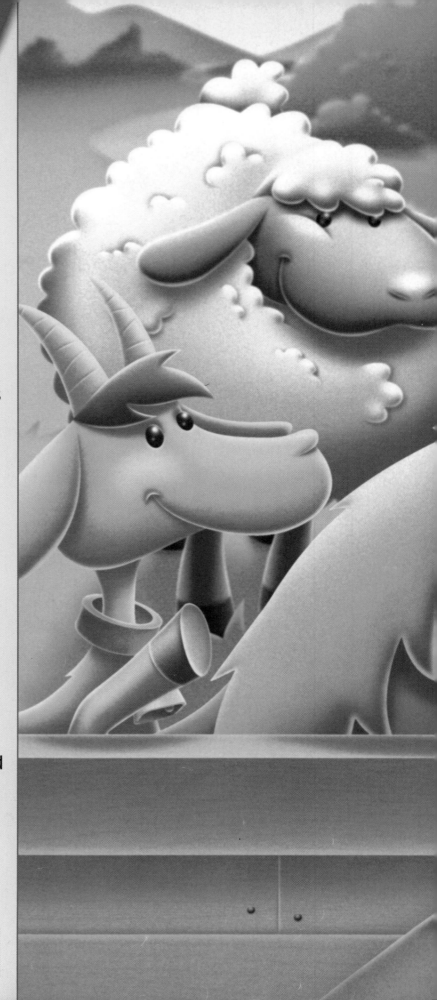

Get Up, Rick!

by F. Isabel Campoy
illustrated by Bernard Adnet

129

Oh, no! It is late!

Where is Rick?

Is Rick sick?

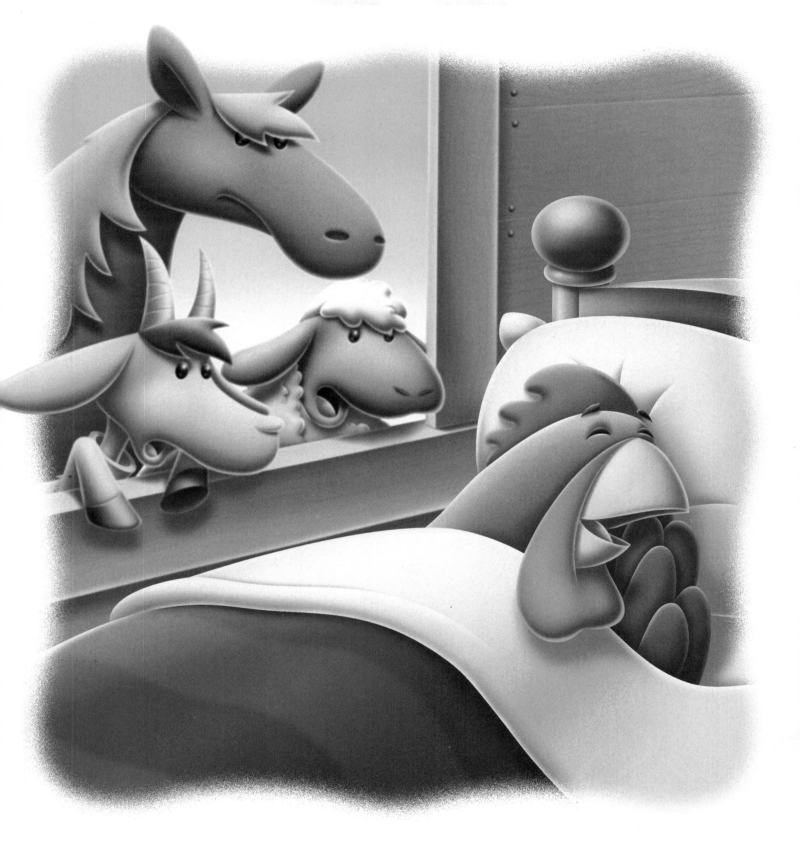

No! Rick is fast asleep!

Get up, Rick! It is late!

Cock-a-doodle-doo!

Oh, Rick, it's too late.

Now Rick is so sad.

We can help Rick.

Let's get him a gift!

What is in the sack?

Will it help Rick?

Yes, it will!

Cock-a-doodle-doo!

Think Critically

R2.2
R2.6
R3.1
W2.1

1 What happens at the beginning of the story? 🌀 BEGINNING, MIDDLE, ENDING

2 How do the other animals try to help Rick solve his problem?

🌀 BEGINNING, MIDDLE, ENDING

3 How does the story end?

🌀 BEGINNING, MIDDLE, ENDING

4 Could this story happen in real life? Why or why not?

REALITY/FANTASY

5 **WRITE** Which part of the story do you think is the funniest? Write about it. ✏️ WRITING RESPONSE

CALIFORNIA STANDARDS
ENGLISH-LANGUAGE ARTS STANDARDS—Reading 2.2 Respond to *who, what, when, where, and how* questions; **Reading 2.6** Relate prior knowledge to textual information; **Reading 3.1** Identify and describe the elements of plot, setting, and character(s) in a story, as well as the story's beginning, middle, and ending; **Writing 2.1** Write brief narratives (e.g., fictional, autobiographical) describing an experience.

144

Meet the Author
F. Isabel Campoy

F. Isabel Campoy lives on a ranch part of the year. A rooster wakes her up every morning. "He doesn't have an alarm clock either!" she says. "I wanted to imagine the opposite situation, and so I wrote about Rick."

Meet the Illustrator
Bernard Adnet

Bernard Adnet grew up in France. As a child, he spent many hours alone drawing, but he also drew for his nieces and nephews. Today he still makes children happy with his drawings.

Connections

Comparing Texts

R2.2
R2.6
R3.3

❶ Look at the roosters in the story and the article. Which pictures do you like best? Tell why.

❷ What things surprised you in the story and the article? Tell why.

❸ Why is it important to help others?

Writing

W2.1

Rick's friends helped him do his job. Think of a time when someone helped you. Write a sentence about it.

My friend helped me with math.

CALIFORNIA STANDARDS
ENGLISH-LANGUAGE ARTS STANDARDS—Reading 1.10 Generate the sounds from all the letters and letter patterns, including consonant blends and long- and short-vowel patterns (i.e., phonograms), and blend those sounds into *(continued)*

Phonics

Make and read new words.

Start with **kick**.

Change the first k to t .

Change t to s .

Change i to a .

Change s to r .

Fluency Practice

Read "Get Up, Rick!" to yourself.
Remember that a comma means to
pause. Then read the story aloud with
a friend. Practice pausing with commas
and end marks.

recognizable words; **Reading 1.16** Read aloud with fluency in a manner that sounds like natural speech; **Reading 2.2** Respond to *who, what, when, where,* and *how* questions; **Reading 2.6** Relate prior knowledge to textual information; **Reading 3.3** Recollect, talk, and write about books read during the school year; **Writing 2.1** Write brief narratives (e.g., fictional, autobiographical) describing an experience.

149

Contents

Lesson 5

1 Decodable Story

Jobs
by Anne Mansk
illustrated by Sachiko Yoshikawa

2 Genre: Realistic Fiction

Dot and Bob
by David McPhail

Trees Help

3 Genre: Nonfiction

151

Phonics
Words with short
vowel o

Words to Know

Review

no

help

what

do

good

Jobs

by Anne Mansk

illustrated by Sachiko Yoshikawa

Dad has a job.

Dad digs and fills pots.

Don has a job.
Don can help Dad.

Mom has a job.

Roz has no job.

Roz can not help.
What job can Roz do?

Roz got a job.
Good job, Roz!

Focus Skill

Characters

The **characters** in a story are the people or animals in that story.

Look at this picture.

The children are the characters.

CALIFORNIA STANDARDS
ENGLISH-LANGUAGE ARTS STANDARDS—Reading 3.1 Identify and describe the elements of plot, setting, and character(s) in a story, as well as the story's beginning, middle, and ending.

Look at the pictures. Point out the characters you see in each one. Tell how you know they are the characters.

Try This!

Look at these pictures. Tell which picture has characters and which does not.

 www.harcourtschool.com/reading

Words to Know

much

find

thank

CALIFORNIA STANDARDS
ENGLISH-LANGUAGE ARTS STANDARDS—Reading 1.11 Read common, irregular sight words (e.g., *the, have, said, come, give, of*).

Bob is my dog.

Can you **find** him?

Bob helps me so **much**.

Thank you, Bob!

GO online www.harcourtschool.com/reading

Dot
and
Bob
by David McPhail

Realistic Fiction

Genre

A **realistic fiction** story seems like it could happen in real life, but an author creates the story.

Who	Where	What

R3.1

Comprehension Strategy

Recognize Story Structure As you read, ask yourself questions. Who is the story about? Where are they? What is happening?

CALIFORNIA STANDARDS
ENGLISH-LANGUAGE ARTS STANDARDS—
Reading 3.1 Identify and describe the elements of plot, setting, and character(s) in a story, as well as the story's beginning, middle, and ending.

164

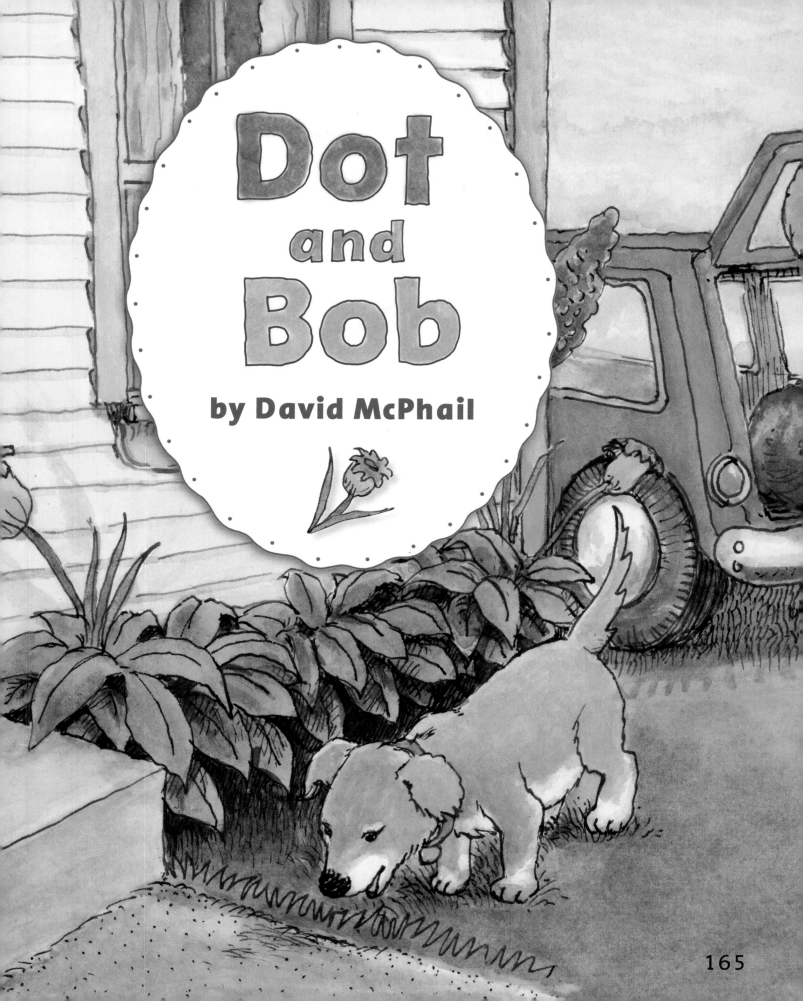

Bob is Dot's dog.
Bob likes to dig.

Oh, Bob! Do not dig there!

Mom has a tree.
Dot will help Mom dig.

It is hot.
It is too hot to dig.

It's not too hot for Bob!

Bob likes to dig.

Bob digs down, down, down.

Did Bob dig too much?

Mom will find out.

Look at the tree top!

Bob kicks and kicks.

Now the tree fits.

Thank you, Bob!

Think Critically

R2.2
R2.6
R3.1
W2.2

1. Who is the character that helps Mom and Dot? CHARACTERS

2. What is the problem with the hole? CAUSE AND EFFECT

3. Who solves the problem? How?

   PROBLEM/SOLUTION

4. Do you think Bob is smart? Why or why not? PERSONAL RESPONSE

5. **WRITE** Would you like to have a pet like Bob? Why or why not? Write about it. WRITING RESPONSE

CALIFORNIA STANDARDS
ENGLISH-LANGUAGE ARTS STANDARDS—Reading 2.2 Respond to *who, what, when, where,* and *how* questions; Reading 2.6 Relate prior knowledge to textual information; Reading 3.1 Identify and describe the elements of plot, setting, and character(s) in a story, as well as the story's beginning, middle, and ending; Writing 2.2 Write brief expository descriptions of a real object, person, place, or event, using sensory details.

Meet the Author/Illustrator

David McPhail

David McPhail started drawing when he was only two. He would draw with a black crayon on paper bags that his grandmother cut up for him. David thought this story was fun to write and draw. "I love how the pictures help a story take shape and make sense," he says.

GO online www.harcourtschool.com/reading

Trees
Help

Nonfiction

Trees Help

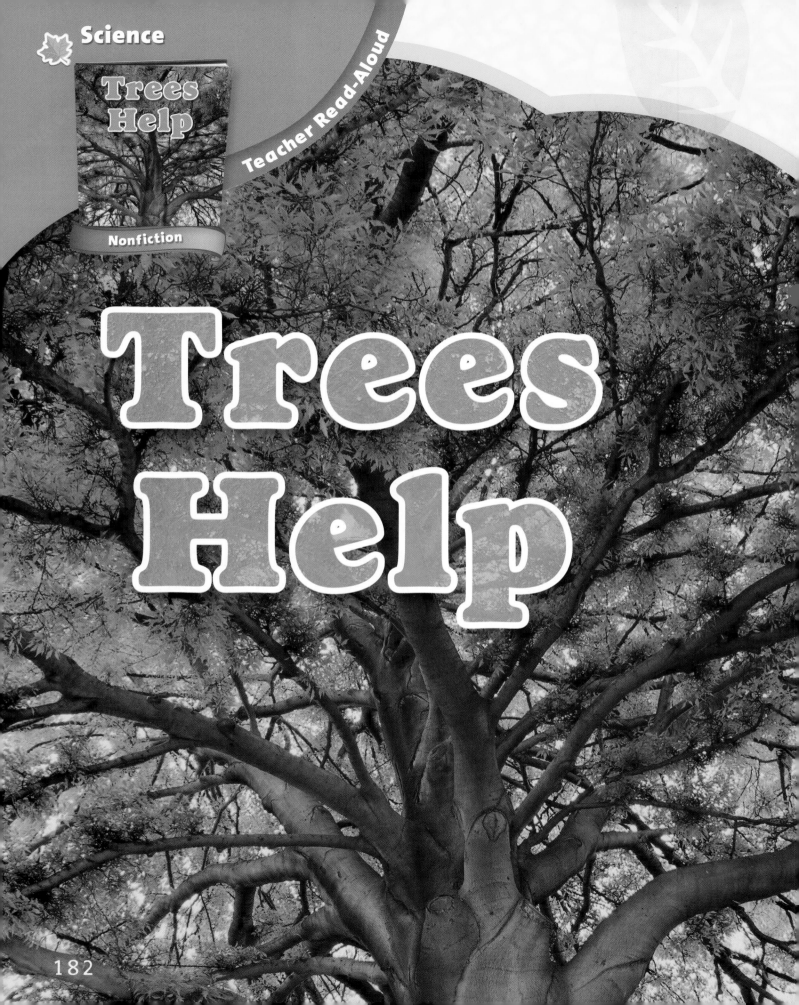

Trees help give us clean air.

Trees are homes for animals.

We use wood from trees.

We eat fruit and nuts from trees.

Connections

Comparing Texts

1. How are the story and the article alike? How are they different?

2. Which pictures did you like best? Why?

3. If you were going to plant a tree, what kind of tree would you plant?

✏️ Writing W2.1

Dot and her dog Bob helped plant a tree. Think about something special you and a pet might do together. Write a sentence about it.

My cat and I could have a picnic.

CALIFORNIA STANDARDS
ENGLISH-LANGUAGE ARTS STANDARDS—Reading 1.10 Generate the sounds from all the letters and letter patterns, including consonant blends and long- and short-vowel patterns (i.e., phonograms), and blend those sounds into recognizable words; **Reading 1.11** Read common, irregular sight words (e.g., *the, have, said, come, give, of*); *(continued)*

Phonics

R1.10

Make and read new words.

Start with **<u>hot</u>**.

Change **h** to **p**.

Change **p** to **d**.

Change **t** to **g**.

Change **d** to **l**.

Fluency Practice

R1.10   R1.11   R1.16

Read "Dot and Bob" with a friend.
Follow along and listen to each
other. Help each other read the words
correctly. If you make a mistake, your
friend should help you. You should
help your friend in the same way.

Reading 1.16 Read aloud with fluency in a manner that sounds like natural speech; **Reading 2.2** Respond to *who, what, when, where,* and *how* questions; **Reading 2.6** Relate prior knowledge to textual information; **Reading 3.3** Recollect, talk, and write about books read during the school year; **Writing 2.1** Write brief narratives (e.g., fictional, autobiographical) describing an experience.

Contents

Lesson 6

1 Decodable Story

A Tall, Tall Wall
by Deanne W. Kells
photographs by Steve Williams

2 Genre: Nonfiction

All on the Map
by Lucy Floyd
illustrated by Max Grover

Roads
by Elizabeth Spires
illustrated by Sachiko Yoshikawa

3 Genre: Poetry

STORE

Phonics
Words with <u>all</u>

Words to Know

Review

where

finds

she

for

up

A Tall, Tall Wall

by Deanne W. Kells
photographs by Steve Williams

Dad has his map.
Where is the wall?

Pam finds it.
She calls Dad.

It is a tall, tall wall.
It is a rock wall.

Dad packed a lot.
It is all for Pam.

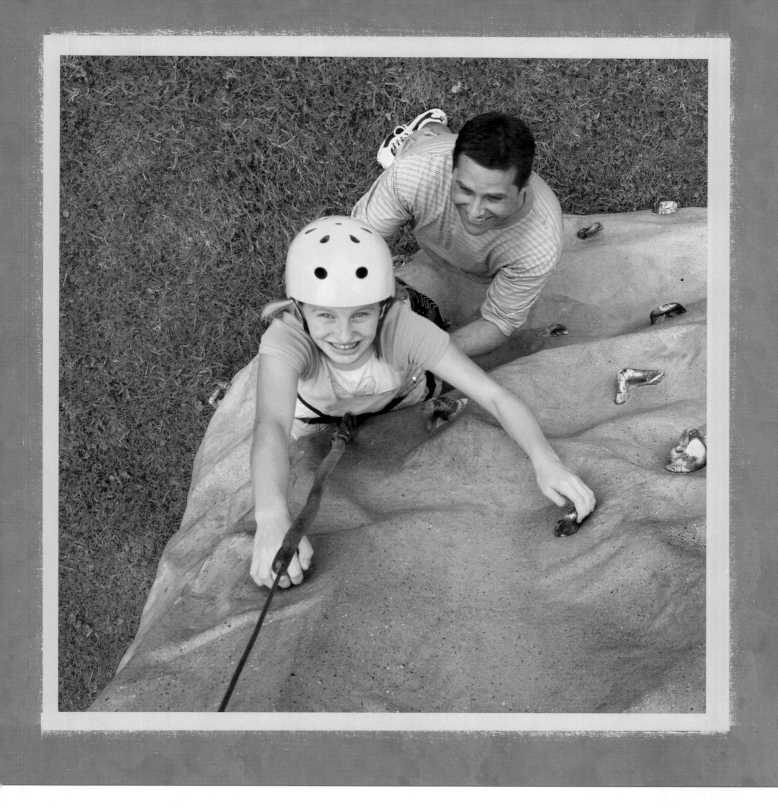

Dad has locked Pam in.
Pam will not fall!

Pam zips up the tall
rock wall.

Pam is on top!

Phonics Skill

Words with <u>all</u>

You have learned about spelling patterns. You can see the spelling pattern **ap** in **cap** and **map.**

Another spelling pattern is **all.** By itself, **all** is a word. Add the letter **h** to the beginning of **all** and you get another word. The new word is **hall.**

Say the picture names. Run your finger under each word. Look and listen for **all.**

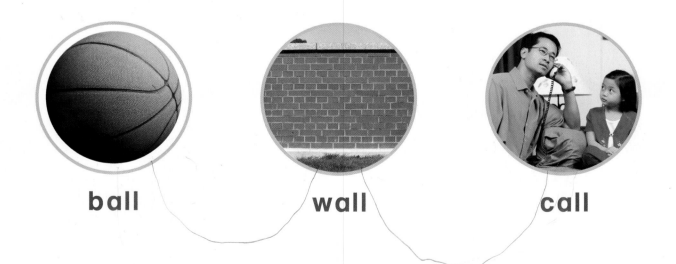

ball   wall   call

196

CALIFORNIA STANDARDS
ENGLISH-LANGUAGE ARTS STANDARDS—Reading 1.10 Generate the sounds from all the letters and letter patterns, including consonant blends and long- and short-vowel patterns (i.e., phonograms), and blend those sounds into recognizable words; **Reading 1.15** Read common word families (e.g., -ite, -ate).

Read each sentence. Choose the picture that goes with the sentence.

1. It is tall.

2. It will fall.

 www.harcourtschool.com/reading

Try This!

Read the sentences.

This is a tall wall.

The ball is in the hall.

We all like the mall.

Words to Know

some

make

of

how

CALIFORNIA STANDARDS
ENGLISH-LANGUAGE ARTS STANDARDS—Reading 1.11 Read common, irregular sight words (e.g., *the, have, said, come, give, of*).

I see **some** hills.

I can **make** a map.

All **of** the hills are here.

Look **how** I did it!

GO online www.harcourtschool.com/reading

by Lucy Floyd
illustrated by Max Grover

Nonfiction

Genre Study
Nonfiction selections give information. Many nonfiction selections use photographs.

Photos	Maps

Comprehension Strategy
Monitor Comprehension: Adjust Reading Rate It is important to understand what you read. Reading more slowly may help you understand the information in a nonfiction selection.

All on the Map

by Lucy Floyd

illustrated by Max Grover

Here is a big town.

Here is a map.

Here is the town hall.

Find the hall on the map.

The town has lots of land.
It has some hills.

Can you find the hills?

Look at how tall they are!

They are on the map, too.

What is this called?

It is on the map.
Can you find it?

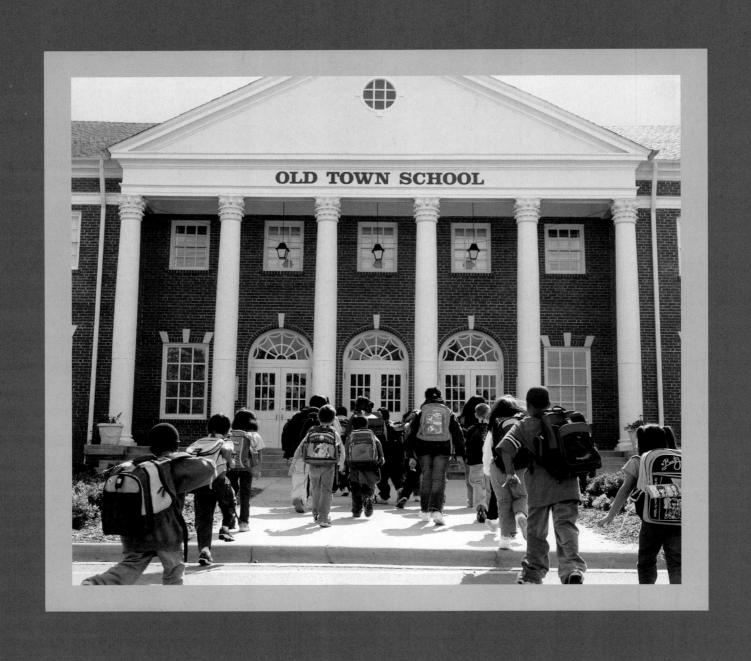

Some kids go here.
What is it?

Find it on the map.

They all like maps!
Now they will make a map.

Here it is!
You can make a map, too!

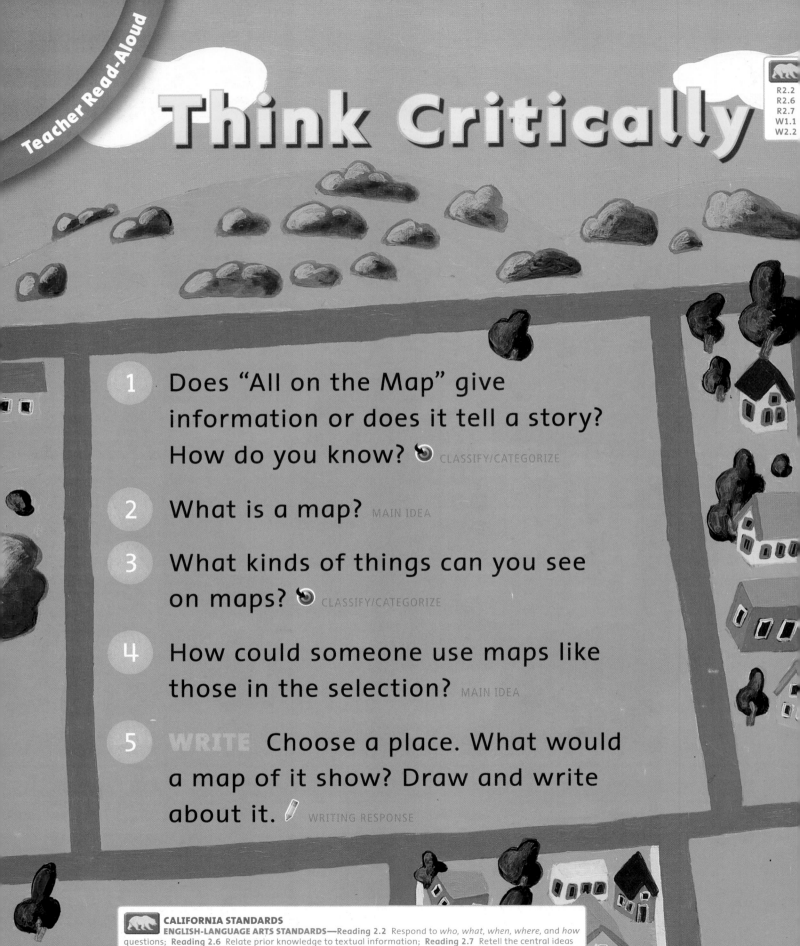

Think Critically

R2.2
R2.6
R2.7
W1.1
W2.2

1 Does "All on the Map" give information or does it tell a story? How do you know? CLASSIFY/CATEGORIZE

2 What is a map? MAIN IDEA

3 What kinds of things can you see on maps? CLASSIFY/CATEGORIZE

4 How could someone use maps like those in the selection? MAIN IDEA

5 **WRITE** Choose a place. What would a map of it show? Draw and write about it. WRITING RESPONSE

CALIFORNIA STANDARDS
ENGLISH-LANGUAGE ARTS STANDARDS—Reading 2.2 Respond to *who, what, when, where,* and *how* questions; **Reading 2.6** Relate prior knowledge to textual information; **Reading 2.7** Retell the central ideas of simple expository or narrative passages; **Writing 1.1** Select a focus when writing; **Writing 2.2** Write brief expository descriptions of a real object, person, place, or event, using sensory details.

Meet the Author
Lucy Floyd

Lucy Floyd has written many stories. Some are make-believe. Some are about real people doing real things. "I enjoyed writing this story," she says. "It reminded me of trips I have taken. Pictures on a map helped me find things."

Meet the Illustrator
Max Grover

Max Grover enjoys painting pictures, because he loves trying out new colors and showing the world the way he sees things. "I enjoyed illustrating this story because I love maps," he says. "I like the colors of maps and the squiggly outlines of roads."

Roads

by Elizabeth Spires
illustrated by Sachiko Yoshikawa

North, south,
east, west,
we run along
and never rest.

Where are we going?
Everywhere!
We never stop
until we're there.

Connections

Comparing Texts

R2.2
R2.6
R2.7
R3.3

1 How do roads and maps help us get where we are going?

2 What do you like best about each selection? Why?

3 Do you think big rig drivers use maps? Why do you think that?

Writing

W2.1 W2.2

Think about "All on the Map." Now think about places near where you live. Write a question that a visitor might ask you.

What is your favorite place to eat?

CALIFORNIA STANDARDS
ENGLISH-LANGUAGE ARTS STANDARDS—Reading 1.10 Generate the sounds from all the letters and letter patterns, including consonant blends and long- and short-vowel patterns (i.e., phonograms), and blend those sounds into recognizable words; **Reading 1.16** Read aloud with fluency in a manner that sounds like natural speech; **Reading 2.2** Respond to *who, what, when, where,* and *how* questions; **Reading 2.6** Relate prior knowledge to textual information; *(continued)*

Phonics

Make and read new words.

Start with **hall**.

Change **h** to **m**.

Change **m** to **t**.

Change **t** to **w**.

Take away **w**.

Fluency Practice

Read "All on the Map" with a friend. Remember that an exclamation point shows strong feeling. Help each other read the sentences with the feelings that best match the story.

Reading 2.7 Retell the central ideas of simple expository or narrative passages; **Reading 3.3** Recollect, talk, and write about books read during the school year; **Writing 2.1** Write brief narratives (e.g., fictional, autobiographical) describing an experience; **Writing 2.2** Write brief expository descriptions of a real object, person, place, or event, using sensory details; **Written and Oral English Language Conventions 1.4** Distinguish between declarative, exclamatory, and interrogative sentences.

Glossary

What Is a Glossary?

A glossary can help you read a word. You can look up the word and read it in a sentence. Each word has a picture to help you.

gift   **She has a big gift.**

dad   **Dad** can help me play.

dig   She can **dig.**

dog   The **dog** sat.

down   Pam fell **down.**

gift   She has a big **gift.**

help   Liz can **help** Ann get up.

hills The **hills** have big rocks.

hold I can **hold** Dad's hand.

home   This is my **home**.

hot   The pan is **hot**.

kick   I can **kick** the ball.

kids   The **kids** ran.

L

late   Oh, no! I am **late!**

M

map   This is a **map.**

N

no   **No**, you can not go out.

S

sack   This **sack** can hold a lot.

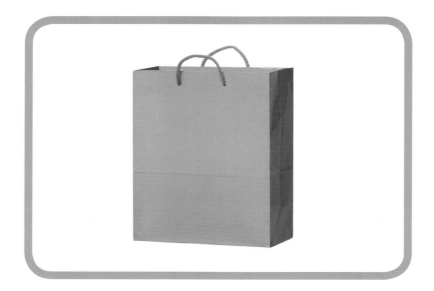

sat   Tim **sat** down.

sick   Jack is **sick.**

van   **Let's get in the van.**

Decodable Stories Word Lists

The following words appear in the Decodable Stories in Book 1-1.

Lesson 1   "Tag"

Word Count: 21

High-Frequency Words	Decodable Words*	
who	**can**	**Pat**
	Dad	**ran**
	Dan	**Sam**
	Pam	**tag**

*Words with /a/a appear in **boldface** type.

Lesson 2   "Sad, Sad Dan"

Word Count: 30

High-Frequency Words	Decodable Words*	
look	**a**	**has**
	am	**hats**
	at	I
	bags	**mats**
	cat	**Pam**
	Dan	**sad**

*Words with /a/a appear in **boldface** type.

Lesson 3   "Miss Jill"

Word Count: 36

High-Frequency Words	Decodable Words*	
have	a	**it**
let's	**big**	**Jill**
now	**bins**	**kids**
the	Dan	**milk**
	fill	**Miss**
	fit	**rig**
	has	**sip**
	in	**sits**
	is	**will**

*Words with /i/*i* appear in **boldface** type.

Lesson 4   "Pick a Sack"

Word Count: 33

High-Frequency Words	Decodable Words*	
have	a	**kick**
too	and	**Mack**
	gifts	**Nick**
	has	**pick**
	his	**sack**
	it	**sacks**
	Jack	

*Words with /k/*ck* appear in **boldface** type.

Lesson 5   "Jobs"

Word Count: 42

High-Frequency Words	Decodable Words*	
do	a	has
good	and	**job**
help	can	**jobs**
no	Dad	**Mom**
what	digs	**not**
	Don	**pots**
	fills	**Roz**
	got	

*Words with /o/o appear in **boldface** type.

Lesson 6   "A Tall, Tall Wall"

Word Count: 58

High-Frequency Words	Decodable Words*	
finds	a	map
for	**all**	not
she	**calls**	on
the	Dad	packed
up	**fall**	Pam
where	has	rock
	his	**tall**
	in	top
	is	**wall**
	it	will
	locked	zips
	lot	

*Words with -all appear in **boldface** type.

CALIFORNIA READING

English-Language Arts Content Standards

1.0 **Word Analysis, Fluency, and Systematic Vocabulary Development**
Students understand the basic features of reading. They select letter patterns and know how to translate them into spoken language by using phonics, syllabication, and word parts. They apply this knowledge to achieve fluent oral and silent reading.

Concepts About Print

1.1 Match oral words to printed words.

1.2 Identify the title and author of a reading selection.

1.3 Identify letters, words, and sentences.

Phonemic Awareness

1.4 Distinguish initial, medial, and final sounds in single-syllable words.

1.5 Distinguish long- and short-vowel sounds in orally stated single-syllable words (e.g., *bit/bite*).

1.6 Create and state a series of rhyming words, including consonant blends.

1.7 Add, delete, or change target sounds to change words (e.g., change *cow* to *how*; *pan* to *an*).

1.8 Blend two to four phonemes into recognizable words (e.g., */c/a/t/* = cat; */f/l/a/t/* = flat).

1.9 Segment single-syllable words into their components (e.g., cat = */c/a/t/*; splat = */s/p/l/a/t/*; rich = */r/i/ch/*).

Decoding and Word Recognition

1.10 Generate the sounds from all the letters and letter patterns, including consonant blends and long- and short-vowel patterns (i.e., phonograms), and blend those sounds into recognizable words.

1.11 Read common, irregular sight words (e.g., *the, have, said, come, give, of*).

1.12 Use knowledge of vowel digraphs and r-controlled letter-sound associations to read words.

1.13 Read compound words and contractions.

1.14 Read inflectional forms (e.g., *-s, -ed, -ing*) and root words (e.g., *look, looked, looking*).

1.15 Read common word families (e.g., *-ite, -ate*).

1.16 Read aloud with fluency in a manner that sounds like natural speech.

Vocabulary and Concept Development

1.17 Classify grade-appropriate categories of words (e.g., concrete collections of animals, foods, toys).

2.0 Reading Comprehension
Students read and understand grade-level-appropriate material. They draw upon a variety of comprehension strategies as needed (e.g., generating

and responding to essential questions, making predictions, comparing information from several sources.) The selections in *Recommended Literature, Kindergarten Through Grade Twelve* illustrate the quality and complexity of the materials to be read by students. In addition to their regular school reading, by grade four, students read one-half million words annually, including a good representation of grade-level-appropriate narrative and expository text (e.g., classic and contemporary literature, magazines, newpapers, online information). In grade one, students begin to make progress toward this goal.

Structural Features of Informational Materials

2.1   Identify text that uses sequence or other logical order.

Comprehension and Analysis of Grade-Level-Appropriate Text

2.2   Respond to *who, what, when, where,* and *how* questions.

2.3   Follow one-step written instructions.

2.4   Use context to resolve ambiguities about word and sentence meanings.

2.5   Confirm predictions about what will happen next in a text by identifying key words (i.e., signpost words).

2.6   Relate prior knowledge to textual information.

2.7   Retell the central ideas of simple expository or narrative passages.

3.0 Literary Response and Analysis

Students read and respond to a wide variety of significant works of children's literature. They distinguish between the structural features of the text and the literary terms or elements (e.g., theme, plot, setting, characters). The selections in *Recommended Literature, Kindergarten Through Grade Twelve* illustrate the quality and complexity of the materials to be read by students.

Narrative Analysis of Grade-Level-Appropriate Text

3.1 Identify and describe the elements of plot, setting, and character(s) in a story, as well as the story's beginning, middle, and ending.

3.2 Describe the roles of authors and illustrators and their contributions to print materials.

3.3 Recollect, talk, and write about books read during the school year.

 **WRITING**

1.0 Writing Strategies

Students write clear and coherent sentences and paragraphs that develop a central idea. Their writing shows they consider the audience and purpose. Students progress through the stages of the writing process (e.g., prewriting, drafting, revising, editing successive versions).

Organization and Focus

1.1 Select a focus when writing.

1.2 Use descriptive words when writing.

Penmanship

1.3 Print legibly and space letters, words, and sentences appropriately.

2.0 Writing Applications (Genres and Their Characteristics)

Students write compositions that describe and explain familiar objects, events, and experiences. Student writing demonstrates a command of standard American English and the drafting, research, and organizational strategies outlined in Writing Standard 1.0.

Using the writing strategies of grade one outlined in Writing Standard 1.0, students:

2.1 Write brief narratives (e.g., fictional, autobiographical) describing an experience.

2.2 Write brief expository descriptions of a real object, person, place, or event, using sensory details.

WRITTEN AND ORAL ENGLISH LANGUAGE CONVENTIONS

The standards for written and oral English language conventions have been placed between those for writing and for listening and speaking because these conventions are essential to both sets of skills.

1.0 Written and Oral English Language Conventions

Students write and speak with a command of standard English conventions appropriate to this grade level.

Sentence Structure

1.1 Write and speak in complete, coherent sentences.

Grammar

1.2 Identify and correctly use singular and plural nouns.

1.3 Identify and correctly use contractions (e.g., *isn't, aren't, can't, won't*) and singular possessive pronouns (e.g., *my/mine, his/her, hers, your/s*) in writing and speaking.

Punctuation

1.4 Distinguish between declarative, exclamatory, and interrogative sentences.

1.5 Use a period, exclamation point, or question mark at the end of sentences.

1.6 Use knowledge of the basic rules of punctuation and capitalization when writing.

Capitalization

1.7 Capitalize the first word of a sentence, names of people, and the pronoun *I*.

Spelling

1.8 Spell three- and four-letter short-vowel words and grade-level-appropriate sight words correctly.

1.0   **Listening and Speaking Strategies**

Students listen critically and respond appropriately to oral communication. They speak in a manner that guides the listener to understand important ideas by using proper phrasing, pitch, and modulation.

Comprehension

1.1   Listen attentively.

1.2   Ask questions for clarification and understanding.

1.3   Give, restate, and follow simple two-step directions.

Organization and Delivery of Oral Communication

1.4   Stay on the topic when speaking.

1.5   Use descriptive words when speaking about people, places, things, and events.

2.0   **Speaking Applications (Genres and Their Characteristics)**

Students deliver brief recitations and oral presentations about familiar experiences or interests that are organized around a coherent thesis statement. Student speaking demonstrates a command of standard American English and the organizational and delivery strategies outlined in Listening and Speaking Standard 1.0.

Using the speaking strategies of grade one outlined in Listening and Speaking Standard 1.0, students:

2.1   Recite poems, rhymes, songs, and stories.

2.2   Retell stories using basic story grammar and relating the sequence of story events by answering *who, what, when, where, why,* and *how* questions.

2.3   Relate an important life event or personal experience in a simple sequence.

2.4   Provide descriptions with careful attention to sensory detail.

Acknowledgments

For permission to reprint copyrighted material, grateful acknowledgment is made to the following sources:

English-Language Arts Content Standards for California Public Schools reproduced by permission, California Department of Education, CDE Press, 1430 N. Street, Suite 3207, Sacramento, CA 95814.

HarperCollins Publishers: "Wag, Hop, Hide!" from *Good for You!* by Stephanie Calmenson, illustrated by Melissa Sweet. Text copyright © 2001 by Stephanie Calmenson; illustrations copyright © 2001 by Melissa Sweet. *Margaret K. McElderry Books, an imprint of Simon & Schuster Children's Publishing Division:* Untitled poem (Retitled: "Roads") from *Riddle Road: Puzzles in Poems and Pictures* by Elizabeth Spires. Text copyright © 1999 by Elizabeth Spires. *Scholastic Inc:* "Trailer Truck" from *Truck Talk* by Bobbi Katz. Text copyright © 1997 by Bobbi Katz. Published by Cartwheel Books.

Photo Credits

Placement Key: (t) top; (b) bottom; (r) right; (l) left; (c) center; (bg) background; (fg) foreground; (i) inset.
7 (t) M. L. Campbell/SuperStock; 8 (inset) Digital Stock/Corbis; 24 (t) Cathy Crawford/PictureQuest; 45 (br) Cathy Crawford/PictureQues; 59 (b) Scientifica/Visuals Unlimited; 60 (t) Telescope; 75 (r) Mike Falco/Black Star; 76 (b) Alaska Stock Images; 77 (tr) Ilene MacDonald/ Alamy; 77 (tl) RM (c) Ray Manley/ SuperStock; 78 (t) Telescope; 81 (br) Stockdisc/SuperStock; 82 (bg) Guenter Rossenbach/zefa/Corbis; 90 (t) Robert Pernell/Shutterstock; 90 (bl) Corbis; 90 (cl) Graham Prentice; RF/Shutterstock; 90 (bc) Lara Barrett/Shutterstock; 91 (tl) Emilia Stasiak/Shutterstock; 91 (cr) Marc Dietrich/Shutterstock; 91 (c) Paige Falk/Shutterstock; 92 (t) Corbis; 92 (c) Ken Davies/Masterfile; 98 (bg) Reza Estakhrian/Stone/Getty Images; 100 (bg) Ken Davies/Masterfile; 111 (cr) Stockdisc/SuperStock; 112 (t) M. L. Campbell/SuperStock; 115 (bl) SuperStock, Inc.; 126 (t) Uschi Hering/Shutterstock; 144 (br) David Toerge/ Black Star; 145 (cr) Jennifer Bruce; 151 (br) Masterfile Royalty Free; 160 (c) Dynamic Graphics Group/IT Stock Free/Alamy; 161 (c) 4x5 Coll-Jon Smyth/SuperStock; 161 (tr) Marvin E Newman/Photographer's Choice/ Getty Images; 161 (tl) Michael Newman/PhotoEdit; 161 (tc) Photofusion Picture Library/Alamy; 161 (bc) PureStock/SuperStock; 162 (t) PhotoDisc/ Getty Images; 162 (t) Telescope; 180 (bc) Rick Friedman/ Black Star; 182 (c) Brian Lawrence/SuperStock; 183 (t) Greg Probst/PictureQuest; 183 (b) Hein Van den Huevel/zefa/Corbis; 183 (cl) Ingram Publishing/ SuperStock; 183 (cr) MedioImages/Getty Images; 184 (t) Telescope; 196 (bc) Plainpicture GmbH & Co. KG/Alamy; 196 (cr) Swerve/Alamy; 197 (tc) Andre Jenny/Alamy; 197 (tr) Beateworks Inc./Alamy; 197 (br) Khoo Si Lin/Shutterstock; 197 (tl) Peter Gridley/Photographer's Choice/Getty Images; 198 (t) Chris Bence; RF/Shutterstock; 201 (bg) Jim Wark/AirPhotoNA.com; 202 (c) Jim Wark/AirPhotoNA.com; 204 (c) Jeff Greenberg/PhotoEdit; 206 (c) Rudi Von Briel/PhotoEdit; 208 (c) Jim Wark/AirPhotoNA.com; 210 (c) David Young-Wolff/PhotoEdit; 212 (c) Will & Deni McIntyre/Corbis; 217 (bl) Chris Bennion/Black Star; 217 (tr) Mike Maloney / Black Star; 220 (t) Cristian Marin/Shutterstock. All other photos © Houghton Mifflin Harcourt Publishers.

Illustration Credits

Cover Art; Laura and Eric Ovresat, Artlab, Inc.